Praise for *The 1.... ...on*

'At its heart a dark, tender and beautifully wrought study in male desperation.'
Time Out

'A triumph . . . . . . it's Marber's night. At 50, he has found his voice again, and it roars.' *Daily Telegraph*

'Patrick Marber's beautiful play never budges outside the tatty old changing room of a non-league football club. But it slides its way into all sorts of emotional territory, exploring paternity, belonging, pain and lost: lost years, lost potential, lost purpose. This is a tender, very touching play about hope and, above all, talent – that rare and fragile flash of genius – and why we prize it so.' *Financial Times*

The Red Lion

Patrick Marber was born in 1964. He lives in London with his wife and their three sons.

PATRICK MARBER

The Red Lion

FABER & FABER

First published in 2015
by Faber and Faber Ltd
74–77 Great Russell Street
London WC1B 3DA

Reprinted with revisions, 2015, 2017

Typeset by Country Setting, Kingsdown, Kent CT14 8ES
Printed in England by CPI Group (UK) Ltd, Croydon CRO 4YY

A CIP record for this book
is available from the British Library

978-0-571-34571-7

2 4 6 8 10 9 7 5 3

This play is dedicated to Steve Ibbitson

Acknowledgements

My grateful thanks to my friends and former colleagues at Lewes Football Club: Charlie Dobres, Ed Ramsden, Kevin Brook, James Boyes, Stuart Fuller, Alex Leith, Ben Ward and Nick Williams.

This play is not about Lewes FC. But it came to be written because my oldest son Albie and I happened to sneak into their ground one summer's day in 2009 and I fell for the club and got involved. The people and the atmosphere of that place inspired much of the feeling of this play. So thank you to all the Rooks.

Rufus Norris, Tessa Ross and Ben Power showed faith in me when I was down. They encouraged me back to the National – the theatre I love and where I began. I thank them for that. It meant more than I can say.

Finally, Ian Rickson coaxed the words out of me and kept me steady – every step, for three years. He made this play happen. And then he brought it home. Thanks, Boss.

PM, May 2015

The Red Lion was first presented in the Dorfman auditorium of the National Theatre, London, on 3 June 2015. The cast was as follows:

Yates Peter Wight
Kidd Daniel Mays
Jordan Calvin Demba

Director Ian Rickson
Designer Anthony Ward
Lighting Hugh Vanstone
Sound Ian Dickinson
Music Stephen Warbeck

Stage Manager Joni Carter
Deputy Stage Manager Maddy Grant
Assistant Stage Manager Constance Oak
Staff Director Anna Girvan

The Red Lion in this revised version was first presented at Live Theatre, Newcastle, on 6 April 2017. The production transferred to Trafalgar Studios, London, where it premiered on 1 November 2017. The cast was as follows:

Yates John Bowler
Kidd Stephen Tompkinson
Jordan Dean Bone

Director Max Roberts
Designer Patrick Connellan
Lighting Drummond Orr
Sound Dave Flynn
Producers Live Theatre and Trish Wadley

Characters

Yates
an old man

Jordan
a young man

Kidd
somewhere in between

THE RED LION

Time

Three Saturdays in winter

One: Noon
Two: Dusk
Three: Night

Place

A semi-professional football club in the south of England.

The play is set in the home dressing room. The room is shabby but fit for purpose. It has been refurbished a few times since the late-nineteenth century but there should be remnants of the past still present.

High ceiling, two windows overlooking the pitch. Rough linoleum floor. Long wooden benches. A line of iron hooks screwed into painted battens along each wall. A treatment table. A Belfast sink with a single brass tap. A small mirror over it. A low fridge. A large built-in storage cupboard. A small, square table. A whiteboard. A cork notice board. A single-bar electric heater mounted high on a wall – its orange glow.

A doorway leads off to an unseen bathroom with showers, WC and a single tub.

Elsewhere, a door leads to the outside. The door has an external sign fixed to it; the sign reads HOME.

One

Noon.

Empty stage.

A single bag on one of the benches. Above it a black trench coat on a hook.

Offstage, from the bathroom, sound of a shower running.

Yates in his club tracksuit and trainers. His initials, 'JY', in white letters on the track top.

He takes a team shirt from a laundry basket and starts to iron it – inside out.

Once the shirt is ironed he turns it right way round and kisses the badge.

Then he puts the shirt on a hanger.

During the act Yates hangs each ironed shirt (sixteen in total) on separate hooks along the dressing-room wall. Badge facing in. Numbers showing, '1' to '17' (but no '13' shirt).

The shower stops running. Kidd enters from the bathroom.

He wears flip-flops and a smart white bathrobe with a hotel logo on the breast. A tube of shower gel in the pocket.

He takes his mobile from the other pocket, checks a text message, curses briefly.

Then he sends a quick one back.

Kidd goes to the whiteboard and rubs out a player's name.

Kidd holds his hand out. Yates gives him a key and continues to iron.

Kidd opens a large cupboard and takes out his suit. He takes it over to his bag on the bench and hangs the suit on a hook.

Yates gestures. Kidd hands him the key.

Kidd paces a bit – in thought – then looks out of the window from where he can see the pitch. He stares out.

Kidd From up here . . .

From *here* . . .

You'd think it was emerald.

You get down *there* . . .

It's a knackered old meadow.

It's not *true*.

Can't play on that.

You can play.

But you can't *play*.

Need it thick and short. Need it to *skim*.

> *He makes a skimming sound and motions with his hand. He stares out of the window, shakes his head.*

He is sanding the goalmouth. He is sanding the bog he made himself.

Ken.

It's amateur.

Eh?

Yates looks up.

I talk to him, 'Hello, Ken, can you *help* me here? Can you give me a surface?'

He says he's on it.

What's he on?

He *mows* – does pretty stripes and circles – motors about, fat arse wedged in his 'ride-on' mowing *tartan*. But he don't do the graft.

He needs to get out there with some *seed*. Chemicals. Fertiliser. Fuck knows – *he* should know!

Kenneth.

Eh?

Yates stares at Kidd.

You ever seen Ken with a fork? Have you ever seen him fork the pitch?

Yates He's a volunteer.

Kidd So?

Yates He's been groundsman fifteen years. Unpaid. Does it for love.

Kidd Can't he love the pitch a bit?

Pause.

Yates It's a plague pit.

Kidd looks at Yates.

It's a burial ground.

You got twenty thousand bodies under there.

Pause.

Kidd Well, I'm staggered it drains so well. Fact it drains *too* well. It's rock on the flanks, do their hamstrings. Cheers, Ken, you dozy div.

He takes out a washbag and goes to the sink. He starts to brush his teeth.

Loves a pint does Ken. A good old 'drink up'. In the club bar with the old soaks – the experts – all yakking about formations: 'See at this level, I think the lads would be more comfortable with a fluid 4–4–2.'

'Oh, dead right, *Kenners*, you're spot on there.'

Fuckin' yard of ale.

He returns to the bench and starts to get dressed.

What would help is if the pitch was used less.

Yeah, great. 'Women's football.' 'The Ladies.'

Kidd dresses, Yates irons.

Yates You ever watched 'em?

Kidd I'm busy Sunday mornings, see me kids.

He observes Yates working.

You watch the Ladies?

Yates I watch all our teams.

Kidd You like the Ladies' game.

Yates They're part of the Club.

Kidd They fuck the pitch. You got them, Youth team, academy – you got the sponsors having a poncey kickabout and little kiddies pissing about in the goals – it mullahs the turf!

Yates Community involvement.

Kidd It's unprofessional!

Yates We're non-league, Jim!

Kidd Yeah, but we ain't a recreation ground! We ain't got *swings*. Ken let his dog on the pitch last week – big black Labrador bouncing about. How do I explain that to my players? Me an' Si and Rodge – we say train – prepare – think – conduct yourselves like *pros*. Oh – mind the dog shit.

Yates I'll talk to him.

Kidd If you would.

Kidd takes a tie out of his jacket pocket. He unfurls it. It's badly creased.

While Yates hangs up another shirt Kidd lays his tie on the ironing board.

Yates returns to the ironing board, stops, sees the tie.

Yates I'm doing the kit.

They face each other.

Kidd It's a club tie. It's *kit*.

Yates thinks a moment then irons the tie.

Obliged.

Kidd finishes dressing, puts on the tie, checks himself in the mirror. Spruces his hair. Then he goes to the whiteboard, starts writing the team out, in formation.

Roberts ain't coming. He's left the club.

Yates Huh.

Kidd Tosser texted me. He's gonna sign up the road. They poached him.

Yates Did Turner up the offer?

Kidd Shoved him another ton a week. I can't compete. I can't make the *moves* on this poxy budget.

Yates Robbo's class, he was always gonna go.

Kidd Get his kit back, yeah? Tracksuit, bag, training top – don't let him nick a fucking thread.

Yates nods. Kidd studies the whiteboard.

That kid . . .

Yates looks up.

You rate him?

Yates Yeah.

Kidd Mmm. He *trains* well. He's a good little *trainer*. But out there . . .?

He shrugs.

Yates places a pair of neatly folded shorts and socks on the wooden bench below each shirt.

Yates How are the kids?

Kidd Eh?

Yates Your children.

Kidd My *kids*?

Yates The ones you made.

Kidd How's *yours*? The fuck is that question?

Yates Innocent one.

Kidd No it ain't, not from *you*.

Yates Fuck off.

Kidd You fuck off.

Yates continues his work. Kidd watches him.

8

My kids are angry and confused. Alright?

He paces, restlessly.

She wants a divorce. 'It don't work. Not for me, personally.' *Personally.*

Yates You said that?

Kidd No, Karen. 'There is a world where this works. But this ain't that world.'

Yates It never is.

Kidd Two years' time you're in the street, see some guy holding hands with your kids, buying them ice cream.
You approach, 'Oh. Hello.' They look at you strange.

You know?

Yates (*softly*) Yeah.

Yates starts to sweep the floor. Kidd walks around, finds a bit of rubbish, kicks it towards the pile Yates is making.

Kidd She's gone *legal.* She's killing me. I got nowhere to go. I'm kippin' on carpets. Phone provider says they gonna chop me off.
(*Takes out his phone.*) I lose this I lose my – my wherewithal. It's a *limb.* I say, 'I *need* it, it's how I conduct my business.'

Yates Can't you . . . 'pay as you go'?

Kidd Eh?

Yates Isn't it a thing . . .?

Kidd It's for infants and drug-dealers. And my former employers – that horrible club – them owners – them millionaire fucking *brewers.* They owe me sixteen grand compensation. Owed it me near three years.

Yates I know.

Kidd They done me, John. Did me like a child. Sixteen grand. I'll *get* it. But they'll settle on the drip when what I need is the *lump*. They promised. Formal handshake. I trusted 'em. Cos they were proper. Cos they spoke nice. What good is a man's word if it's just a fucking sound he makes?

Yates You got debts, Jimmy?

Kidd Who hasn't?

Four kids don't need some deadbeat father.

I ain't cryin about it. I'm just tellin' you.

I could do with some *flow*.

Yates Ask the Board for a loan.

Kidd I did. I'm good for it, John. If you got a bit put by? Some nest egg . . .?

I'm asking you.

They look at each other.

Yates I'm scrapping to pay the rent.

Kidd looks away, in despair.

Yates has finished sweeping. He puts the broom back in the cupboard and takes out a dustpan and brush. He kneels down to the small pile he's made on the floor and gets to work.

Kidd Go on then; today's officials.

Yates Mr Parker, Mr Langley, Mr Sengupta.

Kidd Oh, Mr Parker. 'It Is He Who Cannot See.'

Yates 'He Is The Poor Blind Referee.'

Kidd Yet the man's *hearing* is uncanny. He sent me off, four years back. 'Salty language'. Trophy game, out east.

One of theirs does one of ours. Rakes him. Achilles. Old school. Parker whistles, gives the free kick to *them*! Our lad's stretchered off. I'm in the dug-out. I murmur. I *whisper*: 'You cheat, you blind fucking prick.' Ref's full thirty yards up the pitch. Turns. Straight red. I almost applauded his sensory powers. 'Mr Kidd, I must ask you to leave the playing arena.' *Arena*. Their main stand is a cattle shed. It's chucking it down. Horizontal. I hunch the touchline. Sueders sinking in the mud. Whole ground hating on me. Three hundred pig farmers singing 'fuck off' in various melodies. I show no fear – (*Sticks chest out.*) I'm full robin redbreast. To get out you gotta pass this area – this *latrine* they call a 'family enclosure'. Them lot are the *worst*; all the pubey lads givin' it large, 'Wanker, Wanker.' Some pikey bint fights her way to the front – she gobs on me. She spits on my sleeve! Fucking flob. I keep my shape, politely offer the finger – at which this grandad hurls his pie. I duck, he bellows, 'You gay southern cunt.' Whole families cheering him on.

Yeah, I remember Mr Parker.

You got his biscuits?

Yates Rich tea.

Kidd I thought he liked a ginger?

Yates He used to. He's moved on.

Kidd Ooh, you're good!

Yates It's in the details.

Kidd You and your biscuit spreadsheet. And where's the *harm*?

Yates The man is human.

Kidd He's a human being.

Yates Or so he manifests.

Kidd And if he should unconsciously *favour* us, who's to know of our marginal gain?

Yates We will serve him the biscuit he likes.

Kidd Why serve him the biscuit he does not like?

Yates We're hospitable people.

Kidd It's not a bribe.

Yates It's a courtesy.

Kidd The incremental edge.

Yates Proud tradition of the club.

They chuckle. Kidd studies his team on the whiteboard.

Kidd When you exchange team sheets – if they field that filthy fucking beast –

Yates Donnelly?

Kidd Yeah – remind Mr Parker the big dirty shithouse loves an elbow.

Yates nods.

Prediction?

Yates Three–one, home win.

Kidd We could go third.

Yates Be good.

Kidd Keep this going, we're right in it.

He studies the whiteboard again.

You reckon that kid?

Yates Decent.

Kidd The *pace* on him. The touch. The *caress*.

Pause.

Yates He's coming early. Due now.

Kidd Yeah?

Yates He was a bit tight after training. I said he could have a rub.

Kidd New favourite?

Yates He's a good kid.

Yates puts the ironing board away. He gives the treatment table a wipe, takes out some massage lotions and oils from the cupboard.

Kidd When he comes, gimme five.

Yates nods.

You reckon he's ready?

Yates Yeah.

Kidd Without the loyal 'Robbo' we got room on the bench . . .

Kid won't crumble out there?

Yates Nah.

Jordan appears at the door, carrying his kit bag.

Jordan Shall I come back?

Kidd No, come in!

Yates Alright?

Jordan Yeah.

Yates exits. Jordan looks confused.

Kidd He's coming back.

Jordan stands, a bit awkward.

You can put that on there.

Jordan puts his bag on the bench. Kidd sizes him up.

I been impressed with you. New club, don't know us, learning our *ways*. Kept your head down, bit quiet but good ethic.

And you don't moan. No one likes a moaner. But I gotta be frank, I'm not feeling the *passion*. You wanna have a *kickabout*, there's pub teams. Play five-a-side down the leisure centre. This ain't that.

Jordan I wanna play, boss.

Kidd You wanna play here?

Jordan Yes, boss.

Kidd You wanna play for me?

Jordan Yes.

Kidd Can you be loyal? Because I am demanding. I'm a prickly prick of a person. I'm a bad loser. Losing is an insult. I hate it, I fear it, I dread its dreadful meaning. And when I lose I don't do it graceful. I *howl*. I kick a puppy. I'll kick *you*. You'll think I hate you but I don't. I hate the part of you who's defeated. I hate the inbred piece of you thinks losing's your birthright. You understand?

Jordan Yes.

Kidd To *win*. What a lovely word. It brings us to rest: 'win'.

The will to win. You got that? The guts, do the necessary?

Jordan Yes, boss.

Kidd Men die out there. I saw it once.

He stares at Jordan.

Tell me about your left knee. You protect it. And you do it very clever. Took me an' Si a few sessions to suss it.

Pause.

Jordan I was injured.

Kidd Yes. When?

Jordan I was fourteen.

Kidd Ligaments? Cruciate? What?

Pause.

Jordan A man with a baseball bat.

Kidd Hmm. Why'd he do that?

Jordan He didn't like me.

But it's healed. It was all busted up but now it's healed.

Kidd stares at Jordan.

Kidd Thing is, you say a thing you don't believe.
You can't play you don't trust yourself – trust you're *strong.*

Cos all you are – out *there* – all you are is everything you got.

Some cunt gives you a smack.

In the past.

And I know those men.

I really do.

But you ain't no use less you brave. No use at all.

He looks Jordan in the eye. Jordan might be about to cry.

Don't blub. This ain't the place. You keep it together.

Pause.

Jordan Yeah.

Kidd Alright?

Jordan Yeah.

Kidd Good boy. You strong?

Jordan I won't let you down.

Kidd No, you won't. I'm gonna start you on the bench.

Jordan Thanks, boss!

Kidd We're over budget. If you get on I'll slip you thirty quid – call it expenses.

Jordan . . . OK.

Kidd Out my pocket. Don't tell *no one*. Me and you.

He stares at Jordan until he nods his assent.

You *dazzle*. Then we can talk about a little wage. Legit, through the books. Maybe even a contract. You fancy that?

Jordan Yes, boss, I'd like that.

Kidd Goodo. Take the '17'.

Jordan approaches the '17' shirt. Stops.

Jordan Can I wear the '14'?

Kidd Don't be silly.

Jordan I like that number.

Kidd It's not on offer!

Jordan Please. I had a vision. Last night. I saw myself in the '14'.

Kidd Is this a religious thing or a drug thing?

Jordan Religious. I'm a Christian.

Kidd Jesus Christ wore '14'? Oh, I offend you?

Jordan *Yes.*

Kidd Get over it.

Jordan (*forcefully*) I believe, boss. You don't like it thass alright. But I believe in God and I love him.

Kidd Where you trot off on a Sunday is not my biz. But *here*, you're in *my* chapel.

Have you got a problem with authority?

>   *Pause.*

Jordan Yeah.

Kidd Yeah what?

Jordan *Boss.*

Kidd Is it a long-term problem?

Jordan I think it might be.

Kidd Well, I got the same. Whoever got some hold over me, I wanna kill.

But needs must.

Eh?

>   *Jordan nods. Looks down. Kidd lifts the boy's chin, gently.*

>   *They are close. Kidd looks him in the eye.*

Were you unruly?

>   *Jordan nods.*

You get caught?

>   *Jordan nods.*

They lock you up?

After a while, Jordan nods. Kidd holds his look. Keeps his chin up.

'S alright. We've all offended.

The state is not your mate.

They hate us.

But in here . . . it's a jolly old pirate ship.

Eh?

Jordan nods.

We're gonna win this league.

And we're gonna better ourselves.

And we will be blessed. (*Softly.*) Something like grace.

He gives Jordan an affectionate pat, and then hands him the '17' shirt.

Kidd There you go. Well done.

Jordan Thanks, boss.

Kidd Don't thank me, you earned it.

Yates comes in, carrying twenty match-day programmes.

Yates (*to Kidd*) Si wants you. He's setting out the cones.

Kidd You sort this boy? He made the squad.

He exits. Jordan grins at Yates.

Yates Good lad.

Jordan holds up his shirt, showing the number.

It's a fine number. It's a prime number.

Yates goes to his cupboard and rummages around for some kit.

Jordan takes out his phone, starts to text.

Jordan Texting my mum.

Yates Want me to get her some tickets? Player's perk.

Jordan thinks.

Jordan Nah. She won't come. She don't approve. She thinks you're very bad men.

Yates She's right.

Jordan (*shrugs*) She don't know a good man from a bad.

Yates has found a club tracksuit and kit bag. He gives them to Jordan.

Yates You wear this every training session and match day. You forget to wear it, you're fined a tenner. You lose it, I'll fine you fifty quid. If you leave the club you return it. Laundered.

Yates places a match-day programme on each player's spot on the benches. Jordan watches, enjoying Yates's precision, his quiet concentration.

Jordan I prayed last night. I prayed for this.

Yates There is a God.

Jordan There really is.

Yates Well, it's a point of view.

Jordan You looked out for me. These weeks. Kept me honest.

You're a good man. They all say it.

Yates I have a reputation.

Jordan 'Ledge'.

Yates Hmm.

Jordan Don't like praise.

Yates I like it too much.

He taps the treatment table.

And I don't like the word 'legend'. It's bollocks. The club is the legend.

Jordan starts taking his clothes off. Yates goes to the cupboard and takes out some towels, arranges them on the treatment table.

Jordan The boys said you played here. Way back.

Pause. Yates looks at Jordan.

Yates Yeah. I wore the '5'.

Jordan You any good?

Yates You'd know I was there.

Jordan looks at Yates while he works, still curious.

Jordan They said you built the North Stand.

Yates Nah. I played in a game which built it. A couple of years after the Battle of Hastings. And bloody in its way.

Jordan Yeah?

Yates FA Cup tie. We'd scraped through to first round proper. We're playing a team three leagues above us. The game is bigger than Christmas.

'Bout twenny minutes from time one of theirs knees me in the mush. Intentional but ref doesn't see. I'm staggering. Eyes, nose, gob. *Whoosh.* Only blood. A tooth in my palm.

Ref's looking at me, 'Are you sure, son?' Our bench gestures me come off but we've already used our sub.

(*Softly, remembering.*) My wife's there . . . She . . . her hand on her mouth. Other arm . . . she's holding our first born. Our girl . . . a little bundle in a red shawl . . .

It's nil–nil, it's *snowing*. They're killing us – fitter, stronger – we're pegged in, defending our lives. Five to go – some miracle we nick a corner. Boss waves, 'Get up there, boy. Gooo onnn.' I go plodding. I'm *dead*. Pitch is glue. You know? Ball comes over from the corner. A brown bomb. Low and hard. Near post. I dive to this blur, eyes of blood, catch it sweet. *Boof*. Get in. Thing flies so fast no one sees it till the crowd *roars*. I'm on my front, whole team pile on, kissing me, squeezing my nuts, pitch invasion, all the trimmings. The crowd sang my name.

(*Softly.*) That day . . . I was never so loved.

Next round – we got lucky: away draw in the North-East – huge club. We took three thousand up there.

I couldn't play, turns out I'd fractured my jaw. But this game; we got half a massive gate. On the telly. Made this club rich a moment. We lost eight–nil.

Jordan Was it in colour?

Yates The world? It seemed to be. So they built that stand. And still it stands. And it's a good one. But I didn't build it. I did help my Dad do some of the electrics.

Yates points to the treatment table.

Jump up.

Jordan is stripped to his underwear.

Jordan Erm . . . ?

He gestures to his pants.

Yates As you are. Or as you were born.

Jordan Are you a qualified masseur?

Yates Over the last half century, I've seen a thousand penises in here; from the dainty to the dumbfounding. I think I can cope.

Jordan gets on the table wearing his underpants.

Yates starts the massage – back and legs.

Yates Alright?

Jordan Yeah. Thanks.

Yates puts more oil on his hands, works it in.

Yates OK?

Jordan Yeah.

Yates works on the shoulders.

Yates Tension.

Jordan Mmm.

Yates Can't play if you're coiled. Gotta be loose.

Jordan Guy said it me when I was sixteen. 'Unclench the fist. Unload the gun.'

Yates Literally?

Jordan Nah. He was a . . . like a therapist.

Yates Where?

Jordan In this place for very tense kids.

Pause.

Yates To be good, good at anything, you gotta be tight. But to be *great*, you gotta loosen up.

We shall trick you into a state of nonchalance.

Yates continues the massage. Thinks. Lowers his voice.

I was gonna say . . . if you wanted someone . . . for advice. Guidance.

I'm here . . . I'm *around*.

Kid like you. A prospect. Word travels. They descend.
Agents. Scouts. Managers. You know?

I could protect you. Deal with those situations. Look
after your interests . . .

Pause.

Jordan Be my agent?

Yates No. I – I'd just be a feller . . . who's there for you.

They look at each other.

Don't need to tell anyone. Best not to.

Jordan thinks.

Jordan I dunno if I want the complication, you know?

Pause.

Yates Yeah.

Jordan Nothing personal.

Yates Yeah.

Yates continues the massage, furious with himself.

After a while Kidd bustles in and addresses Jordan.

Kidd A thing. Shoulda said. A word about the officials at
this level of the pyramid: a man who can lodge a small
pencil in the top of his sock and then jog about without
dislodging it is a qualified referee. He is scared and
helpless, a baby in black. He needs to be shown the way.
This league you gotta be *canny*. We get promoted, we *rise*,
the world opens its legs. But down *here* we must help the
man in black to *see*. We must lead the poor blind soul
through this overwhelming universe. You get?

Jordan . . . No, boss.

Kidd You get on today, some big bully kicks you; you exclaim, you go down, you show you're hurt. Because you *are*. You get in the box – you feel a nibble, a brush, you sense a presence, you imagine 'contact', you *tumble*. Do it subtle, no leaping. No one shot you. You ain't no *gazelle*.

> *Yates eases off on the massage.*

Throw-ins, fouls, offsides, corners – any decision the ref gotta make, you claim for *us*. Make him *think* for *us*. He's lost. You beckon him to the truth. As we define it. There it is.

> *Kidd makes to exit.*

Jordan I won't cheat.

> *Kidd stops, turns.*

I don't *cheat*.

> *Pause.*

Kidd It's a *team* game.

Jordan I know.

Kidd Team fuckin' game, kid!

Jordan I know that!

> *Yates quietly slips over to the sink, rinses his hands. Watches.*

Kidd Can't play a lad does his own selfish thing.

Jordan I won't dive.

Kidd These *words*.

Jordan I'm not a cheat.

Kidd Did I ask you to?

Jordan No.

Kidd Did I use that word?

Jordan No.

Kidd So?

Jordan Sorry.

Kidd What I invited you to do was to apply game intelligence.

Pause.

Jordan Can I . . .?

Kidd Can you think about it? No. You step up or fuck off. Right now.

Silence. Jordan gets off the treatment table and hands Kidd the '17' shirt.

Thass a shame.

Jordan Sorry.

Kidd Uh-huh.

Now Jordan sadly offers Yates the club tracksuit and kit bag.

Yates makes a slight move but Kidd glances at him. Yates stays put.

Jordan starts to put his own clothes on. Track bottoms, a sweatshirt.

Kidd You reckon yourself? Too super-talented to play non-league?

Jordan No.

Kidd You might be half decent but you ain't the bollocks, boy. You wouldn't be *here* if you were. But there is a road *out* of here; you play for me – play *with* me – I will show you to some *glory*. I can change your life. This is a step to another step up.

Jordan (*passionately*) I won't cheat, I won't lie, I won't *fake*. Not for you, not for no one! I mean to *stand* for something – you got it, mister? All my life they tell me what to think and to feel and to do but no one – *no one* knows what I feel – sometimes *I* don't know. You don't get to mess in this maze I got. You ain't my father – you ain't my boss – you got nothing I need. Show me *beauty* – give me what's true and tender and real. You don't get to play with my morals just cos I wanna play. Fuck you and your slyness. Don't tell me to be strong – GIVE ME SOME STRENGTH.

Kidd OK. One: no, not my job, you find it in *you*. Two: chill the fuck out. Three: shut the fuck up. And four: listen. We are winning here! Eight games unbeaten – I've built a miracle – a winning *team* – and I'm picking *you*! Cos me, Si, Rodge, Yatesy – *my* team – we've noticed you can kick a ball about in a delightful fashion. We think you have heart and intelligence. We believe you might be a *footballer*. A real one. We talk about kids like you and we gurgle with joy. In three hours' time a contest will be staged out there. Seven hundred people will pay cash money to observe a spectacle of aggression, technique and guile. BE IN IT!

You know that word?

Jordan I know that word.

Kidd The word 'guile'.

Jordan I know it!

Kidd So get involved! *Belong!*

Do what I say: play for the team, win the game.

Our supporters – this club – your *team*. They will *love* you – if you let them.

Don't be the fuck-up. Be the one who makes it throug

You're gonna say 'yes' so let's not drag it out.

Jordan glances at Yates who remains inscrutable. Then he looks at Kidd.

Jordan Alright.

Kidd Good lad.

Jordan Yeah.

Kidd We're good.

They shake hands. Kidd raises his eyebrows to Yates and exits.

Silence. Jordan thinks a while.

Jordan Did you cheat?

Yates I cheated, I lied and I conned anyone I could. I terrorised the young, kicked shit out the old. And I went looking for it.

In my defence, I was a deranged young man.

But *you* . . . don't lower yourself. Don't do a thing you don't believe in.

 Yates holds his look. He lets Jordan settle a moment and then taps the treatment table again.

Jordan You know this man . . .

Yates Jimmy.

Jordan Is he all that?

Yates I work for him. He's my boss.

Jordan I saw a picture down in that bar. You *were* the boss.

Yates Twenty years ago. For two seasons.

Jordan Still . . .

He removes his clothes, climbs back on the treatment table.

Yates I took us down. Lowest points total in the club's history. People who loved me couldn't look at me.

Took me ten years show my face again . . .

He continues the massage.

All that season in here: 'Do this, track this one, you tuck in if he goes. We can get out of this, lads. We won't be *relegated*. Believe, boys, *believe*!'

And other horseshit from the same yard.

'Keep going, lads, keep going.' I'd do this –

He makes a gesture of energy and uplift.

They look away. Don't believe in you. Why should they?

To lose them . . . like drowning . . . and lose yourself . . .

You're an old fool. You're the plague.

Pause.

Jordan You gonna answer my question?

Yates Jimmy Kidd knows how to win. Don't need to agree with the man to be on his team. In this room: *loyalty.* Rest of the world go fuck itself.

Yates continues the massage in silence.

Jordan The boys said you played pro.

Yates Old Division Three.

Jordan Yeah?

Yates For two seasons. Loved it.

(*Shrugs.*) But I was a journeyman. All heart . . . no touch.

I ended up here. Dug in.

My dad played years for this club. He could play a bit.

I used to come in here half-time, eight years old, bring the oranges . . .

Those men. Giants. All hair and cock and laughter.

The pips and peel on my plate.

'Thanks, kid.'

Terrified.

Longing for their approval. To be those men.

Their secrets . . .

And the holy reek of them: sweat and liniment and dubbin.

Fags and talc and booze.

'Alright, John Junior.'

To be the kid . . .

To *play* . . .

(*Nods.*) That's my peg.

My father said a football man dies three times:

Once when he's young and sees he's only second rate.

Twice when he hangs up his boots and has to live like the others.

And the third time . . . slow . . . if he falls out of love with the game.

    Yates continues the massage.

OK?

Jordan (*slight pain*) Mmm.

Yates Here?

Jordan Lower.

Yates (*of the knee*) Bit swollen.

Jordan 'S alright.

Yates continues in silence. Finally, he taps Jordan.

Yates You're done. You warm up good and strong. Keep these loose.

He goes to the sink, washes his hands.

Jordan Reckon I'll get on?

Yates You might. I'll nudge him.

Pause.

Jordan Can I tell you something?

Yates The kit man is a priest.

Jordan He's paying me. Said he'd find me thirty quid. He said don't tell no one. Call it expenses. Thass not right. Is it?

Pause.

Yates What else d' he say?

Jordan He banged on about losing. Bit fuckin' out there, you know?

Yates Oh yeah. He's that. Styles himself a maverick. Likes a *preen*.

He lives for the cameras. But round here, they are scarce.

Jordan gets up from the treatment table, stretches a bit. Yates puts the towels in a laundry basket, the massage oils back in his cupboard.

Yates They'll be coming in. Soon enough.

*Jordan starts putting his kit on. Yates takes out the
warm-up tops, hangs one on each hook. Jordan
watches him, intently.*

Jordan What's your cut?

Yates Eh?

Jordan Before. Thing you said. What would you *take*?

Yates shakes his head.

Everyone wants a cut.

Yates I don't.

Jordan . . . You . . . ?

Yates No.

Pause.

Jordan No take?

Yates No. I'd . . . you know . . .

Jordan You'd . . . ?

Yates Yeah.

Pause.

Jordan You'd do it for love?

Yates The honour. I believe in you.

Jordan You do?

Yates Yeah.

Pause.

Jordan You'll look after me?

Yates Yes.

Pause.

Jordan You got a deal, mister.

He offers his hand, Yates shakes it.

Home team.

Jordan hugs Yates. Yates is overcome, he breaks, hands Jordan a training top.

Jordan Thanks, boss.

Yates Easy. Jim's the boss.

Jordan gets his boots out, starts to loosen the laces.

What are those?

Jordan Shit boots. You gonna get me a sponsor?

Yates When you play like a young god.

Pause. Jordan watches Yates. Thinks. He flexes his leg, wants to tell Yates something . . .

Don't take his money.

Jordan It's thirty quid.

Yates When he comes to pay you, say you can't take it.

Jordan Why?

Yates Principle. The club should pay you. Not him. Keep it *clean*.

Jordan All right.

Yates Let him know who you are.

Jordan Who I am is broke.

Pause. Yates offers Jordan a twenty-pound note. And then a ten.

No – I wasn't asking – I can't.

Yates I'm a billionaire. Pay me back when you're flush.

Jordan nods, takes the cash.

Jordan Thank you.

Yates goes to his cupboard, takes out a mop and a packet of rich tea biscuits.

Yates Ref's due. I gotta slop out his lair. Keep them limbs nice and easy.

Jordan Always loose.

Pause. They look at each other.

Yates See you on the park.

Yates exits.

Jordan sits back on the bench, luxuriating a moment.

Then he goes to the window. Looks out.

He returns to the bench and unzips a pocket in his bag.

He pulls out a syringe and loads it from a small phial.

He straightens his left leg. Then he injects himself just above the knee.

Two

Dusk. Some weeks later.

Heavy rain.

*After the match. Dirty kit flung on the floor. Empty
plastic bottles. Shin pads. Sock tape. Bandages. Mud.
A subs board.*

*Kidd enters – black trench coat over his suit. He wears a
fedora or something similar.*

*He quickly looks around, then hurries into the bathroom.
He returns and takes out his phone – a cheaper model
than the one he had before.*

He makes a call.

Kidd (*in phone*) Mac? Jim. It's a new num— No, keep
the old – I'm between *providers*. Between – yeah. I'm
talking to him *now*. He's standing right next to me. I
know – I'm on it.

    *Yates hurries in, huddled, coat over his tracksuit.
    Soaked and cold.*

    Kidd immediately exits to the bathroom, still talking.

Yeah – all over it – I know – Yeah yeah yeah –

    *Yates opens his coat and takes out the pint he's been
    protecting, a wrapped bag of chips and a large saveloy.
    He puts them on the table.*

    He takes off his coat, shakes it out, hangs it up.

*He takes a glug of his bitter. Then he stands on a
bench, reaches up, warms his hands on the wall
mounted heater.*

*He contemplates the room and the work he must
now do.*

*He opens his chips. Eats. Drinks. Yates has the pint in
his hand as Kidd comes in from the bathroom.*

Yates Guilty.

He puts the glass down.

Kidd How many times? Place – of – work.

Oh. Enjoy your bloody pint.

Yates drinks.

You seen the kid?

Yates In the office. He's having a chat with *The Herald*.

Kidd He's doing *press*?

Yates Charlie H. wanted an interview. Man of the match.
Want some?

Kidd takes a few chips. Paces about.

*Yates goes to his cupboard, takes out a bottle of
ketchup, adds it to his chips.*

*Kidd takes his hat off. Shakes it. Carefully brushes it
down.*

Kidd Do I look a tit?

He puts the hat back on.

Yates Twirl.

Kidd does so.

You look immense.

Kidd puts his hat on a hook. Yates starts to tidy the room. This will occupy him throughout the act. He starts by sorting the wet, muddy kit into three baskets: shirts (all turned inside out), socks, shorts.

Kidd Reckon he'll be long?

Yates Ten minutes.

Kidd takes his coat off, shakes it out, hangs it up. Warms his hands.

Kidd I need a bath. You stick the immersion on?

Yates exits to the bathroom. Kidd paces, takes a few more chips.

What a super game of semi-professional football!

Yates (*off*) Yeah!

Kidd Oh, my former club. Them *brewers*. Enjoy the spanking, did ya? Enjoy your education by a tactical *maestro*? Ha ha! (*Calls off.*) I hate to gloat but tell me I was *regal* out there?

Pause.

Yatesy?

Yates (*off*) You were regal!

Kidd We buried 'em. We funeraled the fuckers. Ha ha!

He takes a can of Diet Coke from the fridge.

Yates (*re-entering*) I had a drink with their kit man, even he said we're playing some.

Kidd Oh we're playing *symphonic*. Feel it.

They both feel it a few seconds. Then Kidd turns to Yates, significantly.

Yates No, Jim!

36

Kidd Whadidisay? Did I speak?

Yates busies himself with work.

Yates It's a 'no', Jim.

Kidd Come *on*! You saw him play today?
Did you see him? The cherub who bossed the game?
Did you attend a football match this afternoon?
Am I all alone in some other world?

Yates Yeah.

Kidd You saw?

Yates Yes.

Kidd You say you saw but did you *see*?

Yates I was in the fucking dug-out, of course I *saw*!

Kidd But did you see? Can you still *see*?

Yates I can see!

Kidd Talent. Temperament. Timing.

Yates Is that from a book?

Kidd He's a ghost! He finds space that ain't there. He's
so fucking good he don't exist! He's a young – a young –
a young –

Yates Too soon to say, let him *breathe*!

Kidd Ooh, he's a prince.

Yates He's just a *kid*!

Kidd We knew he was good but this one's a *peach*.
Tell me he's mustard, tell me this kid is *outstanding*.
Say what you say, Ledge. Say that lovely thing you say.

Pause.

Yates He can play.

Kidd There it is: He Can Play. Eh? Can't he? Ha ha! Say it again.

Yates (*smiles*) He can play.

Kidd He – Can – Play! How *much* can he play, John?

Yates I said he can play.

Kidd So help me get him to sign his *contract*! We gotta find him more money! Now saddle the fuck up to the Board and argue the *case*!

Yates I went last week! They said no!

Kidd You have to ask *again* – have to, *have* to – irresponsible not to! My job – my profession – my *calling*, feller – my holy moly *creed*.

Yates I respect your bubbly enthusiasm – now fuck off.

Kidd exclaims with frustration.

Your current overspend is more than a grand a week!

Kidd It's frontloaded – front the fuck loaded – I'm asking a ton more a week to sign the new *Pelé*!

Yates 'New Pelé.'

Kidd Shorthand. Fuck your mockery.

Yates You wanna increase the offer you'll have to *juggle*. Board won't sanction a penny more.

Kidd 'Sanction'? Who *are* you?!

Yates There's no more money! You spent it and then you spent the overspend!

Kidd Fuckin' Dennis out there.

Yates I saw you haranguing.

Kidd Fuckin' Dennis, fuckin' cock.

Yates I don't disagree.

Kidd 'What d'you reckon,' I say. 'What about that beautiful, glorious kid, eh?' Dennis goes, 'Mmm. I can see the logic, but I don't think the Board'll go for it.' I say, 'Yes, but Mr Club Secretary, *you've* watched the boy play these last weeks, you've seen what he can *do*, player like that is an *asset*, he should be *ours*, we gotta lock him down on contract so them vultures up the road can't steal him! A wise football man like yourself, you who have the ear of our distinguished Board –' He chuckles. He fuckin' *chuckles*, Ledge.

Yates Maybe he saw through you?

Kidd D'you know I think he might.

Yates Jim –

Kidd So let's explore another universe –

Yates I live in this one!

Kidd And it's a sorry one cos you live in fear! Fuck the Board, fuck the Board, fuck, fuck, fuck the Board! You were a *rogue*, you know how it's *done* – 'sanction'?! Them and Us. Since Time Began. John: Be – With – Us! Now *you* gotta talk to the Board, *you* gotta tell 'em to release the cash – I've tried but they don't seem to like me – it's *baffling*. But you they respect, from *you* they will *listen*!

Yates They don't listen, they humour me!

Kidd Why are you so reluctant to do what you know is *right*?!

Pause.

Kidd shakes his head.

It's a frickin' mystery. Three weeks back: 'Here you go, son. Here's the dream, sign there.'

'Can I think about it?'

'Course you can but think it quick, eh?'

He's *still* thinking! It don't stack up.

Kidd paces in frustration then turns . . .

Someone's got to him.

Yates holds his look.

It's them up the road. That stinking rotten club. *Turner.* First he poached Roberts and now he's gonna poach our boy. They've tapped him up.

Yates Nah.

Kidd No?

Yates How would they get to him?

Kidd Carrier pigeon. Fuck should I know? They induced him with a can of Sprite down the discotheque. Or maybe they *phoned* him?

Yates Nah. Kid wouldn't sign for them.

Kidd And you know this *how*? Some optimistic fucking whimsy? Them up the road are a league above us and they'll double his wage. Your mate Turner's a crafty old cove. Thass why I been begging the Board, 'Get this kid on contract, protect ourselves.' And no one *listens* cos no one believes a thing happens till it *does*. No faith in the manager. When will someone in this world believe in me?! John, go see the Board – they're in there now!

Yates I've been! I told you! THEY SAID NO!

Silence. Kidd stares at Yates a moment.

Yates continues to tidy up.

Kidd checks his phone, quickly responds to a text.

Kidd Long interview. Can't we fish him out?

Kidd looks at Jordan's hook, his club kit bag on the bench. Kidd approaches.

Yates Oi.

Kidd I'm looking for the contract.

Yates Don't touch his stuff.

Kidd Alright. Keep your knickers on.

Yates You want me to talk to him?

Kidd He ain't gonna listen to *you*, he plays for *me*!

Yates continues to clear up. Kidd watches him a while.

Kidd goes to the window. The pitch. One floodlight still on.

My sweet Lord. He's forking the pitch. Ken has got his fork out.

Yates I had a word.

Kidd There it is: influence.

He has a thought, looks at Yates, dismisses the thought. He goes and lies on the treatment table while Yates works.

Did you see the pass for the second goal? Outside of the boot – wrong foot – does he have a wrong foot – fifty yards? Sixty? *Boooom*. Have you *ever*? On this quagmire? Ever? In space, behind the three, in his back pocket. Defender almost dies the ball's so snide. It hangs – hovers – *plummets*. Their keeper goes 'Waaagghh' – he *wets* his goal mouth. Benno don't break stride – even *he* can't miss! They don't run to him, they run to the kid, hoist him up. Kid's like 'whatever' – does it all day. *Expects* to. Them grizzled old pricks in their dug-out, they're lookin' at me, 'What Was *That*?' I'm standing there. (*Folds his arms.*) 'It's called "football".' Ha ha! I tipped my hat – have some *brim* you cunts! He's a *surgeon* – he parts a defence like flesh. And he's *brave*. Eh? Heart of an ox. The kid is a *wonder*. The boy is a *lion*.

Yates I KNOW, JIM! I FOUND HIM!

Silence.

Kidd Eh?

What?

You . . .?

What?

Yates He came to me.

Kidd He *came* to you? Cos my understanding – I'm talking here what I've been *told* . . .

You *found* him?

Yates Yes.

Kidd Cos my understanding is the kid walked in the door. Three months back, he walks in this door says he's looking for a club, who do I speak to for a *trial*. You're in here doing some *ironing* and you give him my phone number.

Pause.

Yates I was waiting for him.

Kidd Excuse me?

Yates He walked in this door. *Someone* – he needed *someone* to be here.

Kidd He walks in the door, you happen to *be* here.

Yates No.

42

Kidd Then *what*?

Are you saying you prayed for him?

Pause.

Yates I was here. He came. And I was here.

Pause.

Kidd Huh.

Hmm . . .

Fact is the boy *arrived*. And we can debate the manner of that 'coming' as we so please. But let's agree he *showed up* – out of the wilderness say, clothed only in a – a – *loincloth* . . .

He paces. Thinks. Stops. Gets it.

Oh, you crazy fucking coot. On which planet do you have the *right*? You're managing him.

Pause.

Yates Yes.

Kidd You work for *me*! You got no business getting into my player! There is a code carved in time's wall – YOU DON'T DO THAT!

Yates holds his ground.

Has he signed something?

Yates No.

Kidd But you're his 'representative?'

Yates It's not official.

Kidd Are you *insane*?

Yates Don't think so.

Kidd You on the take?

43

Yates No.

Kidd You paying him?

Yates I help him out.

Kidd And you've told him not to sign his contract.

Yates nods.

Well, I hate to be a rat but I might have to tell the Board what you've been up to.

Yates Don't, Jim.

Kidd You've betrayed me and the club. 'Ledge.'

Yates bows his head.

Kidd You paying the boy to stroke your ego?

Yates *You* tried to pay him, six weeks back.

Kidd I didn't *pay* him, I slipped him thirty quid expenses!

Yates Which he *refused*!

Kidd *What?* He put the cash in his pocket!

Yates is stunned.

Yeah. He says, 'I can't take this, it's wrong.' I say, 'No it ain't, mate.'

And he thinks and then he takes it, puts it in his pocket. He's a *kid* on the make. That's who *he* is. Why shouldn't he be?

Yates is dazed. Kidd thinks a moment, turns.

Roberts . . .

How come you knew that Turner upped the offer?

You go back years with him . . .

You fixed the deal – for Roberts.

Yates No! I'd never do that!

Kidd So what *did* you do? And don't lie, cos I'll know cos you sweat.

Pause

Yates Robbo came to me.

Kidd Oh, they *all* come to you.

Yates He said he didn't wanna play for you no more. He . . . he wanted my advice.

I put him in touch with Turner.

Kidd Instead of advising one of our best players to be loyal, you offered him to another club.

Yates bows his head in shame.

Yates (*softly*) I wanted Turner's respect. That I was still . . .

Kidd *Yeah*.

He stares at Yates with contempt.

I'm off to the Board. You can fuck off out this football club.

Yates For what? *Guiding* a player, *helping* a player?

Kidd For acting in contradiction to the interests of the football club. For disloyalty and disrespect to the appointed manager of this football club. For getting in the heads of valuable assets to this football club and filling said heads with fairy dust.

Yates Jim. Don't tell the Board. *Please*.

Kidd 'Please' don't cut it.

Yates This is all I got. All I got.

You know it.

Let me sort it. I'll make it right.

Pause.

Kidd You will make it *happen*. You will talk to your boy and get him to sign his contract. *Now.* Or I'll go to the Board and you're finished here. You'll be disgraced.

Pause.

Yates OK.

Kidd Off you go.

Yates doesn't move. Thinking.

Hello?

Oh screw it.

He puts his coat and hat on.

You say your 'goodbyes' to this room. I come back, you're *gone*.

Kidd is about to exit.

Yates Why was Tony Mac at the game?

Pause.

Kidd Who?

Yates Tony Mac.

Pause.

Kidd Was he?

Yates You spoke after.

Kidd Don't think so.

Yates You and Tony Mac. Little chat out the car park.

Kidd Not me.

Yates I saw you. Him. And your hat.

Kidd So?

Yates He's a scout. Of sorts. A fixer. Well connected. A man you're desperate to impress. The man who can help you *rise*.

He was here today . . . and he was here two weeks ago.

You want the boy on contract cos you've lied to Mac that he is.

Pause.

Kidd Good stab. Then what?

Yates You *need* him on contract so you and Mac can sell him.

You want to sell the boy. At a price. You dirty fuck.

You'll take a cut of the transfer fee, bung a bit to Mac. He'll do the same his end, shove some to you. Take it both ways.

Kidd Sounds like a plan.

Yates It's what you do. You sell our children.

You prefer to nick a few grand than keep a good player?

Kidd He was never gonna *stay*. Soon as he started *shining* we were never keeping him!

Yates *I* could keep him here!

Kidd It's not your business to!

Yates You don't even *want* to win the league?! We're *second*, we can win it!

Kidd Course I want to! Mac reckons we'll get twenny grand for him – it's a *gift* for the Board, it buys me favour. Then I can get 'em to up the weekly – pay two or three new players. He's not the *difference*, I can win it without him.

Yates He's *our* player!

Kidd I gotta squad to look after. He makes 'em feel *ordinary* – bad for team spirit.

Yates The players love him!

Kidd NO, YOU DO!

You got some *thing* going with him, thass sweet – thass fuckin' *weird*, but no matter. This is a piece of *business*. The club acquires assets and sells or disposes of them as it deems appropriate. I *manage* that. It's my *job*.

Your job is to wash and press the kit.

Back in the day – your imagined day – all looking out for each other – *community* – cheers – this ain't that.

John. You drink too much. You think too much. You feel too much.

I'm selling the player.

Yates *No*. You're in *my* club.

This is my room.

The boy ain't going nowhere. He *belongs* here!

They face each other. A long look.

Kidd Nobody owns him, John.

Yates You go to the Board, I come too. I'll tell 'em every crooked thing you do.

Pause.

Kidd Let's be gentlemen. Let's be sporting: we let *him* decide.

48

He comes in, we tell him the truth and we let him choose his future.

Your way or mine.

Yates considers the proposal.

Yates Alright.

Kidd Done.

He starts to undress to take a bath. Yates stands, thinking. Troubled.

Hang on. Why don't you *want* the kid on contract? Playing for the club you love?

Yates refuses to answer. Starts to tidy up. Kidd shrugs, continues to undress.

Yates stops his work, turns to Kidd.

Yates I do want him on contract. But not to you.

Pause.

Kidd You never approved of me – day one – and I've *tried*. I came in two years back to a losing club. This was a morgue. Now we're buzzing. I give my all but it's never enough for you.

The Ledge loves *everyone* . . .

Except me.

Why? What've I gotta do?

He is now stripped to his underwear.

Yates Kiddo . . .

Kidd Say it. I'm a man. Why d'you hate me?

Pause.

49

Yates Because you've got no manners. You never say 'please' or 'thank you'. You got a mouth like a potty. You've got the worst disciplinary record of any manager in this league. It *shames* us. You never notice the volunteers who make this club possible. You've got no interest in the *life* of the club. You corrupt the players. You rob them of their innocence. You're selfish. You're a liar. You're a user. So determined to get on you're not even here. Everywhere you go it ends ugly. You drive the club mad till it's a relief to pay you off. Anything to be rid of you. You're a thief, Jim. From a family of thieves and drunks. You did well to dodge the drink. You don't love this club or any club. You don't even love the game. You're the plague.

Kidd smarts, wounded.

Kidd That's clear.

He puts on his white robe and exits to the bathroom. Sound of water running.

Kidd re-enters, stands in the doorway.

He stares at Yates while he works. After a while, Yates turns.

I saw you play once. I was this . . .

He holds his hand three feet off the floor.

My dad brought me here. He was a cruel judge of a player. But now and then he'd come up here, just to watch *you*. No one else. He loved you. Any game, big game, nothing game . . . He said, 'You watch this feller driving his team on, you *notice* this man who would die out there. As if he longed for it. As if his life depends on the commitment he makes.'

In our house, you were famous. Any of us, 'See, what you need more of, *boy* . . . what you need, *girl*, is the spirit *he's* got. You wanna *be* something in this world, go find in yourself what Johnny Yates is made of.'

I was fifteen, I said, 'Dad, it's a lovely sentiment but you're an alcoholic postman. You're a depressed and disappointed pisshead who can't control himself.'

He gave me a right old smack.

And I was gone.

Yates Jim . . .

Yates approaches but Kidd backs away and sits on a bench, head in hands.

Jordan enters, wearing his club tracksuit. Yates gives him a look. Jordan exits.

I shouldn't have spoken.

Kidd I *asked* you. It's alright. I know what this job is. I got the courage to be despised.

And I . . . John . . . I . . . am going places. All the way. I'm going there.

Yates Who's coming with you?

Kidd looks up at Yates.

You don't have to be alone.

Kidd The manager handles it. Whatever it is. He stands apart. He's a *fort*. It's my job.

Yates No, it's your choice, Jim.

They look at each other.

Kidd (*softly*) It's ever so lonely here.

Yates I've been there. You won't make it. No one can.

Kidd I will.

He pulls himself together. Stands.

You couldn't manage here – you couldn't *manage* – cos you're soft.

    You're a guy I inherited. You're a mascot. An old man I'm compelled to work with cos of history.

I know your dream: you want me *out*.

And then the Chairman says, 'John. In our hour of need, will you return and lead us to promotion, you and your sweet young prince?'

And there it is: the *glory*.

Not in this life, pal.

    He heads to the bathroom.

Your boy comes in, you keep him here. And we will see where he stands.

    He exits to the bathroom. Turns the taps off, gets in the bath.

    Yates continues to tidy up. After a while, Jordan enters.

Jordan OK?

Yates Yeah.

    Jordan nods offstage to the bathroom. Yates nods.

    Yates goes to the fridge, takes out an ice pack from the freezer compartment, wraps it in a small towel, hands it to Jordan.

Jordan Thanks.

    He sits on the bench, the ice pack held to his left knee.

Yates You speak to anyone after the game?

Jordan No.

Yates No?

Jordan Just a guy with Jimmy. Said I played well. Terry.

Yates Dark blue coat. Grey hair.

Jordan Yeah. *Tony.* Jimmy said there were things we had to talk about.

Pause.

Yates Why d'you take that money off him?

Jordan looks at Yates.

Jordan He wanted me to. I was scared.

Yates It gave him an in. He thinks you're biddable.

Jordan It was thirty quid.

Yates I *told* you.

Jordan You give me cash sometimes.

Yates *I'm* your guy, we're the team!

Jordan I took his money *once*. I needed it.

Yates I bought you them boots. It's what I'm *here* for.

Jordan nods an apology.

Cos he's figured out our . . . thing.

Jordan looks at Yates, worried.

Jordan Am I in trouble?

Yates He doesn't blame you.

Jordan Why would he?

Yates He doesn't.

Jordan You said you'd look after me. Protect me. All the rest: the contract, you and Jim – it's not my business. I just wanna play.

Yates stares at Jordan.

(*Softly.*) You think I'm something special. Want me to be.

But I ain't, John. I ain't all that.

Yates Yes you are.

Jordan You wanna think it.

Yates I believe it.

Jordan Don't make it true.

Yates You're good, son. *Believe.*

> *Yates makes his gesture of energy and uplift then stops himself.*
>
> *Kidd enters, towelling his hair. Jordan conceals the ice pack.*
>
> *Yates continues to tidy up. Jordan sits, waiting.*
>
> *Kidd starts to get dressed. After a while:*

Kidd Ledge. Would you mind giving us a few minutes?

Yates No. We agreed we'd both talk to him.

Kidd (*to Jordan*) Your call.

> *Pause.*

Jordan (*to Yates*) I'll be alright.

Yates No. You won't.

> *Pause.*

Jordan I'll find you if I'm not.

> *Yates stares at Kidd.*

Kidd He hath spoken.

> *Yates exits. Kidd closes the door.*

54

You got yourself in a pickle there. 'S alright. We've all done it.

He's a super fellow. But he's got no business getting into you.

Jordan But you're cool with him?

Kidd *Yeah*.

Jordan It's alright?

Kidd It's gone.

Jordan Cos I love that man.

Kidd I love him too. *Now*, we have a fast-moving situation: you remember that guy? Tony Mac.

Jordan nods.

Me and him have a number of arrangements. He's been talking to another guy at a club. A *big* club – professional – sleeping giant, League One. And this club would like you to go up there for a trial.

Jordan A trial?

Kidd Big step up. Well done you.

Jordan What club?

Kidd A good and reputable club is all you need to know right now. And there are things it's best you *don't* know. I say this to protect you.

Jordan Boss . . .

Kidd We need to establish some parameters for the deal – were it to happen.

Jordan How would the trial work?

Kidd At present we're talking theoreticals.

Jordan *Is* there a trial?

Kidd There *would* be – *if* me and you are in accord.

Assuming we were, you'd take a train to an undisclosed city in the Midlands and lodge with a kindly landlady. You'd work with their first team squad. You'd do your lovely thing. A week or so later, all being well, they'd offer you a contract. Could be four hundred a week, maybe more. You would be a professional footballer. Bingo. A ticket to become someone *magical*.

Don't forget your old chums.

Jordan I – I can't afford the train fare or the landlady thing.

Kidd No, no, no, all the financing is my end.

Jordan You?

Kidd It's not a thing. The thing – the pressing *thing* is we need you to sign your contract *here* so we can get a transfer fee. Without a contract they can sign you on a *free* and we, your friends, don't benefit. You see?

Jordan Almost.

Kidd Mmm. It's delicate. Now be a good lad and fetch your contract.

Jordan hesitates.

Jordan I should talk to John.

Kidd No, you can't talk to *him* cos you're talking to *me*. Get it. Please.

Jordan goes to his bag and finds the contract. He hands it to Kidd.

Now to some people, a contract is a binding legal document.

Jordan Isn't it?

Kidd I think of it as a chip. A position to come from. Its meaning is moot. And I'm not sure it has meaning in the strict sense of the word.

Jordan What word?

Kidd The word 'meaning'.

Pause.

Jordan You want me to sign the contract and then break it?

Kidd He's got it.

Jordan It don't sound right, boss.

Kidd People say, 'You should not break a contract.' And yet and yet and yet, people *do*. The making and breaking of contracts is how life is *lived*. Property, finance, employment, legals, marriage. It's what we *do*. And by 'we' I think I mean the human species. So who is to say what's what in this world? Who are we to judge these people? Who are we to judge ourselves?

Jordan It's complicated.

Kidd It is exactly that. So there are steps we must take and there may be subterfuge.

Jordan But I like it here.

Kidd We like you for liking it.

Jordan I like *playing* here. I love it.

Kidd Son. The Board have instructed me to sell you.

Jordan reacts.

It's not personal, they think you're *marvellous*. But the club needs the money. I've argued and raged. I can't win this one.

Jordan But it's a Board meeting *now*, I could talk to 'em?

Kidd Nooo, you can't go in there!

Kidd's phone rings. He scrambles for it. Answers.

(*In phone.*) Yeh. Now. Any second. Yeah.

He puts the phone in his pocket.

Jordan Would they want me to have a medical?

Kidd Who?

Jordan This other club.

Kidd Is that a problem?

Jordan No.

Kidd You a cokehead? Cos they'll find that shit if you is.

Jordan I don't do coke.

Kidd Of course you don't.

Jordan The Midlands?

Kidd I know you have concerns. But let me walk you through the *maths* and you'll appreciate the upside.

Jordan I dunno, boss.

Kidd *Listen.* So, you trial and they like you. *Then* we can cut a little deal. You, me and them.

Jordan A *deal*?

Kidd Mmm . . .

Jordan About the fee?

Kidd Hmm?

Jordan You're talking about the fee?

Kidd The fee?

Jordan For the transfer?

Kidd No, no, no – something else. The fee is different, the club gets the fee.

Jordan Which club?

Kidd This club, the selling club, who else?

Jordan You said 'them' before.

Kidd When? Who?

Jordan Just then, like a second ago.

Kidd Who said 'them'?

Jordan You.

Kidd Me?

Jordan *Yes*.

Kidd When?

Jordan Just now.

Kidd I said 'them'?

Jordan Yeah.

Kidd I don't think so.

Huh.

To tell you the truth I'm a bit lost here!

Jordan I wanna talk to John. Can I talk to him, please?

Kidd He's gone home. You *can't* talk to him. He's not *entitled* to advise you. You talk to him, the Board kick him out the club. Kill him. You don't want that.

Jordan There's a fee and you said . . . 'something else'.

Kidd There it is. Let's call it a bonus.

Jordan Because it *is*?

Kidd Because let's call it that.

Jordan This is fucked!

Kidd Oi! Sit *down* and *listen*!

Jordan You fuck off, mister! I don't need your shit!

Kidd Yeah you do! Sit down and behave yourself. *This* is the conversation where you become a man who might amount to something.

Pause.

Jordan What's the bonus for?

Kidd The bonus? Why it's a thank you.

Jordan To you?

Kidd Me, you, everyone. Happy days.

Jordan I don't –

Kidd It's a sweetener, common practice. Don't *fret*.

Jordan I need to understand!

Kidd In actual fact, you really don't!

Jordan Who are 'them'?

Kidd Fuck 'them' – we're beyond that!

Pause.

Jordan Do *I* get a bonus?

Kidd Yes you do, innit super? It's so super you don't wanna mention it. It's one of them great things best left unsaid.

Pause.

Jordan How much?

Kidd The figure?

Jordan Yeah.

Kidd Well, it depends on the structure.

Jordan Can't you just *tell* me? Tell me something I can *understand*!

Kidd There's a *number*. I suppose I could tell you that.

Jordan OK.

Kidd The number is seven thousand pounds.

Jordan No shit!

Kidd Innit sweet?

Jordan I get seven grand?!

Kidd Oh, I *wish*.

Jordan But you said –

Kidd What did I say? I said that's the *number*. The *figure*, the figure is something else.

Jordan The total is seven?

Kidd You see *this* is the conversation.

Jordan Yeah. What do I get?

Kidd You get two and a half. Very tidy. Buy a car with that – you'll need it, zip off up the training ground each day.

Jordan Who gets the rest?

Kidd It's really not relevant.

Jordan *Who?*

Kidd 'Other parties to the deal.'

Pause.

Jordan I want five.

Kidd It's not available.

Jordan Five or forget it.

Kidd Five is not a conversation! Not worth our time you gonna fuck about all *naive*. See – me and Tony Mac – we done the *work* here, set it up. For *you*.

Jordan Is it legal?

Pause.

Kidd Is that a serious question? Or something you're saying to pass the time?

Jordan Is it legal?

Kidd Which?

Jordan All of it – *any* of it?

Kidd I don't know. *Is* it?

Jordan I'm asking *you*!

Kidd Am I a lawyer?

Jordan Is it *illegal*? Cos I ain't up for that.

Kidd Well, I know it's not *wrong*.

Jordan Is it a bung?

Kidd No.

Jordan What is it then?

Kidd It's *football*. It's how the poor survive! We're talking 'bout pocket money. The owner of this club, the big fat builder, you know what he's *worth*? You think he cares? We're underlings. *Atoms*. He bought the club so he could *sell* the club. In five years he's gonna flog this ground to the highest bidder. They'll build houses. And a superstore. Councillers, planners, developers – all in it together, all jolly old handshakes and Rotary Club. He'll make *millions*. And then he'll make a few more when he builds this club a crappy new (ha ha) 'community stadium' up near the by-pass. A mean little ground made of breezeblock and tin. And his company will *sponsor* it and *then* he'll launder his cash through the club. It's the wild west down 'ere. Unregulated. Every cunt for himself. It's a bleak English landscape, I know, but there it is.

Jordan I dunno.

Kidd You *need* to know, cos everyone's *poised*.

Would I fuck you?

Jordan No.

Kidd Would I fuck myself?

Jordan No.

Kidd So? You wanna stay *here*? Hundred quid a week and part-timers kicking lumps out you? Some scaffolder going in studs up and the pissy blind shitbag ref never noticing fuck all – the elbows and the knees and the fist in your bollocks? Crappy pitches and cold showers and a Tesco sausage roll after the game? (*Passionately.*) God gave you some brilliance – and now you've got an *out* – TAKE IT! You've *earned* it, you *deserve* it! You can *escape*! There is *nothing* here. You get the fuck out of this place, boy, and don't ever look back.

I want this deal, feller. I ain't gonna lie, I need it – for reasons I hope you never know. But it also happens I want to save your life.

Jordan Why?

Kidd Because it's worth saving. Because it *can* be saved.

Sign this contract – here and now – give yourself a future.

   Pause.

Jordan I gotta talk to the Ledge.

Pause.

Kidd He knows.

He knows enough. Don't talk to him. You talk to him, he's involved.

You understand?

Jordan stares. Desolate.

Jordan Does he get a cut?

Kidd He gets a little slice.

Pause.

Jordan He's cool with it?

Kidd Yeah.

Jordan . . . Huh . . .

Pause.

Kidd You see?

Jordan nods, devastated.

He's happy for you, just can't say it. He set you on your way. Now you're saying 'thank you'.

Jordan He wants me out the club.

Kidd No! He wants you to prosper, to progress. He wants what's best for you. This was always an option. Day you walked in this door. You see? It's really not a thing.

He offers a pen.

The guy's waiting for my word. You're gonna sign this and get up there tomorrow. And who knows? They might be stupid, might not fancy ya. So you come back here and . . . we'll do something else.

Jordan I can't play here, you want me out.

Kidd Don't you get it? You're too good for us.

Pause.

Jordan *John* wants me out. He lied to me.

Kidd Hey. Don't be too hard on the old boy.

You're talking about a – a decent man. And . . . he ain't all there, you know?

Twenny years ago. When he was the boss . . . he took this club down . . . and he . . . well, he lost his way. That season. He couldn't cope.

He lost his marriage, his kids. They moved abroad. They're in New Zealand. He lost his home. All gone. And then he's on the street. He was a . . . homeless. You know?

And he vanishes. Goes missing. For ten years. *Ten* years.

Then he turns up one night. Some hostel in Carlisle. He's all beaten. Can't talk. He's *gone.*

They say, 'D'you know your name?'

All he does is roar. He just . . . *roars.*

So they calm him . . . *Shhh* . . . They feed him and they hose him down . . .

And they see he's got a tattoo on his heart. A red lion. The club crest. This badge.

They call. And three old boys from the Supporters' Club, they go up there and bring him back.

And very slowly, he recovers his marbles . . . and in time, they let him manage the kit.

So you go easy on that feller.

Cos he's been around.

Three

Night. A few weeks later.

Yates stands alone. In his coat.

He takes in the room. It's clean and tidy. Kidd's hat is on a hook. Yates pulls a bottle of beer from his coat pocket, smacks it open at the sink. Drinks.

He stares at the room.

Kidd enters. They look at each other.

Kidd You killed me.

   Pause.

Yates Had to do it.

Kidd Why?

Yates Had to be rid of you.

Kidd Why?

Yates I love the club.

Kidd You *love*?

Yates I love this football club.

Kidd They just let you *go*!

Yates I was disloyal.

Kidd You're finished.

Yates It's a Board decision. I accept it.

Yates goes to his cupboard and opens it. Stuff tumbles out. A ball, pumps, cones, etc. Yates lets them fall, then puts most of the stuff back.

Kidd Where you gonna go?

Yates rummages and pulls out an old kit bag. He searches some more in the cupboard and pulls out his boots, an old trophy, some medals, a framed photo, a soft toy lion. He stuffs them in the bag.

What you gonna do, John?

Yates closes the cupboard, leaving the key in the lock.

That *kid*.

Yates Yeah.

Kidd Did you *know*?

Yates No.

He goes to his kit bag. Finds a screwdriver.

He heads over to his peg and attempts to unscrew it from the wall.

It won't budge. Yates sweats with the effort.

Kidd He's in there now.

Yates looks blank.

In the boardroom. I came out, he's going in.

(*Softly.*) He fucked us.

And now he'll fuck me some more.

Yates has another go at the peg. Kidd paces a little, thinking.

Did you have to tell 'em *everything*?

Yates I answered their questions.

Kidd Loyalty.

Yates I know.

Kidd The dressing room.

IT STAYS IN HERE.

It's the only law.

Yates I didn't volunteer the information. It's a disciplinary. Club business. We misbehaved. We've been punished.

   Pause.

Kidd They've suspended me.

'Pending further investigation into a series of gross misconducts.'

Something like that.

I'm banned from the ground.

I'm . . . *suspended*.

I can't do a thing.

I'm off the *premises*.

Banished.

I'm not allowed to *talk* to my players.

I can't *talk* to a club employee.

Who am I gonna talk to?

Yates You can talk to me.

Kidd (*softly*) They said I'm a crook. In some respects it's not untrue.

But Jesus, I'm small fry.

Chairman said a thing about *fraud*, get police involved.

Yates Get a lawyer.

Kidd I said, 'Guys, I can't *live* on what you're paying me.

Few hundred a week. It can't be *done*, I gotta work the angles.'

John. I put a brick through the Chairman's window. I just smashed his car.

I wish I hadn't.

There's cameras out there.

I fucked myself.

He watches Yates struggling.

What are you doing?

Yates I want my peg.

Kidd watches.

Kidd Fuck sake.

He watches the struggle some more.

Here.

Yates hands him the screwdriver. Kidd has a go. He grunts with the effort.

Ancient frickin' things.

Some cock painted over the screws.

Yates So he did.

Kidd keeps trying.

Kidd I'm gonna try chip the paint off.

Yates Good thinking.

Kidd I'm gonna chip it off with *this*.

Kidd works at the paint with the head of the screwdriver.

He tries the screws again. Struggles.

(*Grunting to heaven.*) Will you grant me the gift of some purchase?

He finally gets some movement.

It's coming! It's turning! Yeeaasss!

He manages to wrench off the peg – but a screw cuts his hand as he pulls it off.

Shit!

He hands the peg to Yates.

Yates Thank you.

Kidd holds his hand up, the blood flows, he heads to the sink to rinse the cut.

Kidd I'm cut. I'm wounded.

He shows his hand.

I'm bleeding . . . Ooh . . . Haaahh . . . Don't like my blood . . . John . . . ?

Kidd is unsteady, could faint. Yates helps him over to the treatment table, sits him down, raises Kidd's arm above his head.

Yates fetches medical supplies. He starts to clean up the wound.

Hey . . . go back in there? Tell 'em . . . tell the Board . . .

Yates Tell 'em what?

Kidd I lose this job. I'm out the game. You get done for 'gross' you're *tarnished.*

Ruined.

I've got children.

Yates wraps a bandage round the wound.

John. Do you miss your kids?

Yates Yeah.

He ties off the bandage.

Kidd I *like* you. Why d'you take against me? We had some laughs. Had some . . . moments. Thoughts. Tactics. Three weeks back, we were hugging on the touchline.

Yates You want a hug, Jim?

Kidd *Please.* Go back in there?

Tell 'em they're wrong. Tell 'em . . . we're top of the league.

Yates stares at Kidd.

Yates I think of those men . . . a dozen men in a room above The Red Lion . . .

In 1892.

They founded a football club.

Not for profit . . . not to further their standing in the town . . .

But to meet a need . . .

That a crowd of people gathered together in support of a team has purpose. *Meaning.*

The game is ritual; made-up rules, man-made oppositions. Make-believe.

The *crowd*, the ceremony, the collusion of souls *willing* it to matter – makes it matter.

Look. This will never happen again. Not like *this.*

Something so pure, so innocent, we forget we have it.

Those men knew. They knew we would need to *yearn* for the sacred.

You and men like you.

You sold out our clubs and you sold out our game.

Kidd I *love* this game! It's my *life*, ya pompous old prick! People *like* the mess of it – they like the biting and fighting and greed – it's *human*! It's not *church*. You're in dreamland. It's *over* – it's not merry old 'association football'. It's a business and nothing – nothing I know in this world stops money. Five, six years they will *raze* your stand. Bulldoze it. You gonna protest on the pitch? You gonna plant yourself there with Ken and Joan and the Supporters' Club? All waving the club's code of conduct like King Canute?

Yates (*distantly*) I'm just a man. I am weak. Give me your strength.

Kidd stares at Yates.

Kidd John, don't go mad, wake up, come back to earth and *spare* me! Go back in there. *Fight* for me. *Please*. Ain't no one else gonna front up for me. I can't *re-train*. I can't work for some *company* – I don't wear a logo – I wear this *badge*. I've got no trade. I'm an idiot. I'm *this*. I live in *here* and out *there* on that beautiful meadow.

There's nothing else.

Jordan comes in.

Jordan (*to Kidd*) They wanna see you.

Kidd Again?

Jordan Yeah.

Kidd *Now?*

Jordan Yes.

Kidd What d'you tell 'em? What *didn't* you tell 'em?

Yates Jim. Remember you're an adult.

Kidd (*to Jordan*) Piece of fucking shit!

Jordan You shut your mouth!

Kidd You fucking Judas!

Jordan approaches Kidd.

Jordan You wanna say that again?

Kidd No, cos I've said it already!

Jordan approaches. Kidd picks up the screwdriver. Brandishes it.

Jordan Oh, thass cool.

Kidd Ledge, you gonna call him off? John? Yatesy?!

Jordan grabs Kidd's arm and twists it behind his back, takes the screwdriver.

Aaarrgghhh!

Jordan tortures Kidd for a few seconds. He squeals in pain.

Jordan pulls Kidd on to the treatment table, pins him down.

His capacity for violence is extreme.

Jordan raises the screwdriver – murderously – to stab Kidd in the face.

Yates (*to Jordan*) Don't do that.

He's beaten. No need to kill him.

Son.

Let him go.

After a few moments, Jordan lets Kidd go. Jordan looks from Kidd to Yates.

Jordan You two. You messed with my head!

Kidd Excuse me? *What?!* Me and him are out the club cos of *you*!

Jordan Yeah, me too – and I'm sorry – but it ain't my *fault*!

Kidd Not your *fault*? I'm sorry, did we force you to go up to the Midlands with a knee full of steroids? Did we inject you with that shit you been using to manage the pain? Might you not – as a *Christian* – have found it in your good Godly heart to confess to your trusting colleagues that you *couldn't* go on a trial cos your leg is swimming with anabolic goat piss?!

Jordan I couldn't think – I lost my way!

Kidd You take a medical you think they ain't gonna *find* it?! You *case*!

Jordan I hoped they might fix it!

Kidd Your knee is fucked, boy!

Jordan I didn't know how much!

Kidd Find a new sport – *snooker*! You keep shooting that shit you won't walk when you're thirty!

Jordan I hoped they might want me enough to *help* me!

Kidd But they didn't!

Jordan I hoped they might find me a specialist who –

Kidd They were angry you wasted their time! They were perplexed – understandably – that the parent club (us) sent them a *cripple* posing as a player! They called our chairman and then they lodged a formal complaint with the FA. You worked a miracle: you stirred our Board to convene a series of emergency meetings. First time they've acted with urgency for a hundred years. You and your gammy leg have brought this club into disrepute. They'll get fined, it'll be in the *Herald*, it's *bad*. You've made us look like amateurs.

Jordan You *are*! Those guys up there – different league!

Kidd Fuck off! OK, we don't do drugs tests but we know our stuff, me and him.

Jordan No, you really *don't*. Those men, they were *pro*. They know this game. The drills and the training, systems, moves, options, fitness, nutrition. You people here – *Old Testament*. They don't tell me to dive, no give you some cash and think they *own* you. They're professional people.

Kidd You *lied* to us! From day one! (*To Yates.*) How can you bear this?

Yates I admit, it's disappointing.

Jordan (*to Yates*) Yeah? You sad you don't get your *cut*? Your little slice?

Yates looks at Kidd, who plays innocent.

He said you were in on it . . .

Yates (*to Kidd*) You told him I was on the take?

Pause.

Kidd Yeah. I know, it's not impressive.

Jordan (*to Yates*) You weren't?

Yates No.

Yates stares at Kidd.

Kidd Yes, you were. You took him from me. You took my boy.

Yates (*to Kidd*) Don't keep the Board waiting.

Kidd takes a look round the room, goes to the mirror, straightens his tie.

Kidd They're gonna fire me. Right now.

I would.

75

I think . . . hmm . . . I sometimes get a bit above myself.
Oh . . . shit . . .

He wipes his eyes. Yates opens his arms.

Yates You'll survive.

Kidd No I won't.

Yates You cheer up now.

Kidd Oh, I'm cheerful.

Yates Always restless. Can't stop to think.

Kidd If I think I'll die.

Yates Have a drink.

Kidd I'm teetotal.

Yates Have a cuddle.

Kidd No thanks.

Yates You ever had a cuddle?

Kidd Never.

Yates No?

Kidd Proud of it.

Yates Not your old mum? Your dad?

Kidd Fuck off.

Yates Couldn't do it, eh?

Kidd I don't remember.

Yates You don't recall it?

Kidd No, mate.

Yates Kids need a cuddle, *all* kids need a little cuddle.

Kidd *I* didn't.

Yates D'you cuddle your kids?

James.

Jimmy Kidd.

Do you love your children?

Have you ever loved a single living soul?

Kidd stands, inconsolable.

Silence.

Then, he gets it together.

Kidd They fire me, fuck 'em. I done it before I'll do it again: kids' team, youth team, pub team, Sunday league, county league, step step step – I'm back.

I am *good* at this game.

He starts to exit.

Yates Kiddo. Your hat.

Kidd stops. Comes back. Takes his hat from the hook.

He holds the hat, looks at Jordan.

Kidd I loved watching you play. Good luck to you.

Jordan nods. Kidd puts the hat on.

John. You killed me. But I forgive you.

Yates Thank you, Jim.

Then slowly, respectfully, Kidd doffs his hat to Yates.

Kidd exits. Yates and Jordan stand in silence.

Jordan I let you down. I shoulda told you I was injured.

Yates nods.

Jimmy said . . . you went right under. Was that true?

Yates Yeah.

Yates thinks a moment and then hands his peg to Jordan.

Would you put this back for me?

Jordan takes the peg over to the wall and starts to screw it back on. Yates turns away, stares out at the pitch.

Jordan I got off the train today.

And I was certain, 'Go missing. Disappear. Never be seen again.'

I couldn't face you. Couldn't face no one. I couldn't bear this life.

I lay outside the station. On the grass. And I imagined it, a long time.

Escape.

He has finished the peg. Yates nods his thanks.

I come home and my mum got herself a new man. They are *doing* it. I'm movin' out. I ain't listening to that.

Yates Mmm.

Jordan You know?

Yates There is no more appalling sound. Reminds us where we came from.

Jordan hands Yates the screwdriver.

Was it your father, broke your leg?

Jordan nods.

They look at each other.

I asked too much of you. I needed too much.

Pause.

Jordan You gonna look for another club?

Yates shakes his head.

You should. You got knowledge. Up there I thought,
'I wish John was here. He'd know the drill. He'd fit in.'

Yates goes to the sink, washes his face.

Yates When I was born.

My mum brought me to the match.

They said, here's a young Lion.

After the game, after a drink . . .

They brought me up here. Bathed me.

He gestures to the sink then dries his hands.

I could play a bit.

Way back when.

He stares at the room. He speaks softly, distantly.

This dreaming game . . .

Seven years old.

Here are my knees.

My boots.

A goal.

I remember.

The sound.

Boof.

Silence.

A cheer.

Is this it? That thing?

Yes! Turning away. Reeling.

Arm in the air, one arm in the air, like my father, like the men I revered, my arm raised, wheeling with joy.

Running, running . . .

I ghost through me.

Vanishing child.

Seven.

To be free.

To be a boy.

Greatness.

Oh.

How would that be?

 Pause.

 They look at each other.

I'll miss the floodlights.

The grass and the boys.

Such light.

You like an evening game?

Jordan I love 'em.

 Yates approaches Jordan. Kisses his forehead.

Yates Look after yourself.

Jordan Always.

 Pause.

If I can play again . . . can I let you know?

 Yates nods.

Will you come and watch me?